Welsh Jokes

Welsh Jokes

Compiled by Wynford M Jones

GEDDES & GROSSET

This edition published 2001 by Geddes & Grosset, an imprint of
Children's Leisure Products Limited

Compiled by Wynford M Jones

© 2001 Children's Leisure Products Limited, David Dale House,
New Lanark, ML11 9DJ, Scotland

Illustrations by Jim Barker

ISBN 1 85534 942 6

Printed and bound in the UK

A miserly old bachelor living on a farm near Aberystwyth was in the habit of visiting a neighbouring farm every Sunday just before lunchtime. Every week, his neighbours would politely ask if he would like to stay for lunch, and every week he would say, "Yes". This went on for many years, but one Sunday, the neighbours were surprised to find the old man was accompanied by a handsome young man. "This is my nephew up from Cardiff," explained the old man, adding, "I promised I'd take him out for Sunday lunch."

Cardi businessman, Guto Griffiths went on a skiing holiday in the Alps and was, unfortunately, buried by an avalanche. As the search party scoured the area, the leader called out:

"This is the Red Cross. Is there anybody there?"

A faint voice, that of Guto Griffiths, was at last heard saying: "I've given already."

A man was explaining to the local minister that one of his parishioners was in serious trouble:

"Ever since her husband died, her debts have gone up and up. She's so far behind with the rent that she's about to be evicted. She'll be out on the street

Jim Barker

with four children under ten."

"Oh, that's tragic!" said the reverend, "I must help her. How much rent does she owe?"

"Nearly a hundred pounds."

"Here, give her this before it's too late."

Then, as an afterthought, he asked: "Are you a relative?"

"No," replied the man, "her landlord."

After the longest engagement in Welsh history, Dai eventually said to Gwladys:

"Don't you think it's time we got married?"

To which she replied: "Who would have us at our age?"

After winning the lottery, a young Cardi lad raced around to his parents' house, already full of ideas as to how to spend the money:

"… and I'm going to buy two cars, a Porsche and a Rolls-Royce, a big house in Tenby and a villa in Merthyr and have a boat and take flying lessons and buy a plane…"

"Hang on, boy," interrupted his father, "… what about me and your mam?"

"I'm going to give you £10 each."

Silence. After a while the son asked his dad what he was going to do with his £10.

"Marry your mother!" came the reply.

A customer enters a bar in Ceredigion, picks up a pint glass, points to a spot about an inch from the bottom of the glass and says to the barman:

"Put beer in up to here, then fill up the glass with water, if you don't mind."

"That's the first time I've been asked for such a drink," said the barman.

"Listen mate," said the customer, "if you had what I had, you'd drink it too."

"Why? What have you got?"

"Twenty pence."

True story: Two locals, Tony and Brian, left Lampeter and travelled by car, plane and taxi to arrive at their destination in Sweden, about 12,000 miles away. They were greeted at the hotel by an English-speaking receptionist who asked them if they had a pleasant journey. Brian replied:

"Not bad. Mind you, we had a bit of snow at 'Tafarn Jem'."

A woman drove a brand new Range Rover on to the forecourt of a car dealer in Aberystwyth.

"I want to sell this car," she said to the salesman. "Give me £15 and its yours."

"£15?" he gasped, "it's got to be worth about £20,000!"

"Listen, love," explained the woman, "I've just come from the solicitor's where he read my late husband's will. Me and the children did all right, but he'd put a clause in saying that his fancy woman should have the proceeds of the sale of his new car."

A Cardi farmer's son gave his English girlfriend an engagement ring with the thinnest possible gold band and the tiniest diamond ever. As she complained, he explained that though it was small, the diamond was flawless.

"No wonder," she observed, "there's no room for a flaw."

Somebody asked Miss Williams why she had never married. She replied:

"I have a dog that growls, a chimney that smokes, a parrot that swears and a cat that stays out all night. Why do I need a husband?"

Whenever the ladies of the chapel came for afternoon tea, the shrewish Mrs Olwen Griffiths ordered her husband into the *cwch dan star* (the cupboard under the stairs). One day, they were discussing how the women handled their husbands. All were fairly strict, but none could compete with Mrs Olwen Griffiths.

"… And not only will he get in there as soon as I tell him to, but when I say

'Come here', he's here in a flash. Just watch. Alfred, come here."

No response.

"Alfred. Come here."

No response.

"Alfred! I order you to come out of that cupboard!" she bellowed.

"No I won't," came the muffled reply, "I'll show you who's boss in this house."

An antique shop in Tregaron, owned by William Williams, had a sign outside it which read:

WILLIAM WILLIAMS

JENWIN ANTEECS

One day, a tourist came into the shop:

"I say, old chap. I must say you've made a terrible hash of the spelling on your sign."

"Oh, is that so?" replied Williams. "Let me tell you something. Every week, at least ten of you English tourists feel you have to come into the shop and point out my bad spelling. On the other hand, once they are in, most of them buy something."

Ianto and Guto, old bachelor brothers from a farm near Corris, decided one day to visit the seaside. They found themselves sitting on the beach at Aberdovey. In front of them, a beautiful young lady was water-skiing, and the two old men watched in amazement. Finally, Ianto turned to Guto and said: "I don't think she's ever going to catch up with that boat."

A scene in a guesthouse near Tregaron at breakfast time.

Guest: "Could we have runny eggs, overdone sausages and bacon, a few slices of old, rubbery toast and a pot of cold, weak tea. Thank you."

Landlady, aghast: "I can't do an order like that!"

Guest: "Why not? You did yesterday."

Overheard at a seance in Boncath…

"Is there anybody there? Knock once for 'Yes' or twice for 'No'."

Three brothers, equally daft, decided to modernise their farm by digging a silage pit. After many hours of backbreaking work, the pit was finished but there was an enormous pile of earth beside it. To get rid of the pile, they dug a big hole, and only when they had filled that hole with pile number one, did they realise they now had a second pile. For several hours they pondered the problem and in the end decided to sleep on it. The following morning, the older two were still at a loss, but the youngest brother announced he had the answer:

"All we have to do is dig another pit, but this time, make it twice as big."

Englishman: "My son was born on St George's Day, so we called him George."

Scotsman: "My son was born on St Andrew's Day, so we called him Andrew."

Hambone: "My son was also born on a special day."

Scotsman: "So you called him David?"

Hambone: "No, Pancake."

A conversation which took place at a meeting of the Free Wales Army High Command:

"What we'll do is declare war on England."

"But we'll get hammered."

"Yes, but when they beat the Germans they gave them billions of pounds to reconstruct."

"True. But what if we win?"

Courting couple, Dilys and Dylan, travelled all the way to Barry Island to visit the fun fair. On their return, Dylan's Mam asked how they had got on. Dylan replied:

"Mam, it was brilliant. We went on everything twice except for the Tunnel of Love. That was a bit of a disappointment."

"Why was that, luv?"

"Well, we got soaked, didn't we?"

"How was that, then? Was the boat leaking?"

"What boat?"

Dic, crossing the street in Corris, was knocked over by a car speeding through the village.

"Why don't you watch where you're going!" shouted the driver.

"Why?" replied Dic, "are you coming back?"

"Oh, Rhys. Shut the bedroom window will you. It's bitter cold outside."

"All right, luv. There, do you think it's any warmer out there now?"

A drunk man in a Swansea bar was going on and on.

"Did you know I can imitate any bird you care to name?" he asked.

"How about a homing pigeon?" said Gwladys the barmaid.

Seeing that his butty was miserable, Bill said:

"What's up Rhys?"

"I got home from work early yesterday and caught the missus in bed with Ianto."

"Good grief! What did you do?"

"Went and made a cup of tea."

"But what about Ianto?"

"He can make his own bloody tea!"

Farmer's daughter, Haf Pryce, was troubled and sought the advice of her friend, Gwladys:

"It's like this see: on Monday afternoon this young man came to the door and asked if Mam and Dad were in. I said 'No' and he took me into the kitchen and made love to me over the table for nearly an hour. On Tuesday he came again, asked if Mam and Dad were in, I said 'No' and for two hours he made love to me on the sofa in the sitting room. On Wednesday, he turned up again. 'Your Mam and Dad in?' 'No'. For three hours we made mad, passionate love in my bedroom."

Gobsmacked, Gwladys could only ask: "So, what's the problem?"

"Well " replied Haf, "what does he want with my Mam and Dad?"

Two old farmers decided to celebrate their retirement by taking their first ever holiday. They decided to go abroad, to England, on a two-week bus tour of historic sites. Half way through the tour they arrived, at lunchtime, at a place called Runnymede. They had a pub lunch and, because the beer was particularly good, the two brothers found it hard to tear themselves away from the bar. By the time they did, the conducted tour had already started, and they arrived as the guide was explaining that at this very spot the Magna Carta had been signed.

"When?" asked Dick.

"1215," replied the guide.

"Damn," groaned Ianto, "missed it by twenty minutes."

Megan: I do hear you is having triplets.
Bethan: Yes, that's right.
Megan: Duw, Duw. That's amazing!
Bethan: Yes. The doctor said it only
  happens once in two million times.
Megan: Good grief! When did you
  have time to do the housework?

It was the first day of work for a shop
assistant in Bala. The manager told her to
add up the till receipts at least three times
to make sure of getting the right answer.

"Did you count it three times like I
said?" asked the manager.

"Yes," she said, "here are the answers."

A retired couple in a North Wales village were pleased when the wife became the "lollipop lady" at the local school. It meant a bit of extra money and would get her out of the house for a while. However, on the first day, she left the house at 8.30 and did not return until 11.15.

"Where on earth have you been?" asked her worried husband.

"You know," she said, "it's taken till now for a car to come along for me to stop."

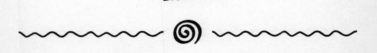

Every Saturday night, Aberystwyth is invaded by the *bois y wellis*, the hambones from the hills. Unable to find the girl of their dreams, they are very soon drunk and ready to take on the world. On one such night, a particularly large hambone charged into a crowd which had gathered outside the kebab and cockle shop.

"Come here, Rhys Morgan!" he shouted, "I'm going to punch your lights out!"

To everyone's amazement, the more he hammered the unfortunate man, the louder the victim laughed.

"What do you find so funny?" screamed the tormentor.

"The laugh's on you, butt," came the reply, "I'm not Rhys, I'm Guto."

Jim Barker

A **young couple lived in a council house in Swansea. It was quite a nice house, but the wife was always going on about moving to a more expensive place. The husband had a good job, but he liked living where they were and that was that, not that it stopped the wife nagging. Then one day, out of the blue, the man came in and said: "You know you're always going on about living somewhere more expensive? Well, you soon will be. The council's putting the rent up."**

A Swansea Jack was trying to persuade a Swansea Jill to let him spend the night with her:

"Oh no. I couldn't let you stay."

"Why not?"

"I'd hate myself in the morning."

"So sleep late."

The Philosophical Society of Upper Corris met to discuss the question:
"IS THERE LIFE BEFORE DEATH?"

Waiting to catch the 4.30 train from Paddington to Swansea, Jack passed the time by having a go on the station weighing-machine. He dropped his 10p in and a disembodied voice said:

"You weigh 12 stone 3 lbs . Your name is Jack. You are from Llanelli. You are waiting for the 4.30 train to Swansea."

Jack pondered how a machine could know all that, then went off to the gents with his suitcase. When he returned he had changed his clothes, brushed his hair forward instead of back and shaved off his moustache. He tried again:

"You still weigh 12 stone 3 lbs. Your name is still Jack. You are from Llanelli. You have just missed the 4.30 train to Swansea."

Glyn Rhys's wife asked him why he no longer brought her flowers and chocolates as he had done when they were courting. The charmer replied: "Would you give a worm to a fish, after you'd caught it?"

Telephone conversation:

"Hello Dai, fancy a pint down the club tonight?"

"Sorry butt, I can't tonight, Berwyn Griffiths is singing in the Brangwyn Hall."

"How about tomorrow then?"

"Sorry, he's singing in St David's Hall in Cardiff."

"What about the weekend then?"

"No chance, I'm afraid. He's doing a

concert in Ponty on Friday and Merthyr on Saturday."

"Hang on, since when have you been a fan of Berwyn Griffiths?"

"Well, actually, I've never hear him sing."

"So why are you going to all these concerts then?"

"I'm not. I'm going to see his wife."

There were only a few eligible women in a small mining village in the Swansea valley and Jack's son, Jacko, was desperate to get married, but every time he told his dad he was thinking of getting engaged, Jack said:

"Sorry son. I'm afraid she's your sister."

One day, Jacko's Mam noticed him moping by the fire and asked him what the trouble was. Jacko explained that Jack seemed to have fathered every girl in the village.

"Don't you listen to that old ram," comforted Mam. "You marry who you like."

"But I can't marry my sister," objected Jacko.

"You won't be," said Mam with a wink, "your dad's no relation of yours."

A man came back from the pub one night with a juicy bit of gossip: "They were saying that new milkman has slept with every woman in this street except one."

"Yeah," replied his wife, unimpressed, "must be that snotty cow in number six."

Jacko, determined to improve himself and get out of the pit, was steadily working his way through the Miners Institute library. His wife soon started to feel neglected as night after night, Jacko did nothing but read. One night she turned on him and said:

"I'm beginning to wish I was a book…"

"So do I," he said, "at least I could change you once a week."

Two young lads from a very rough estate in the Rhondda were killed when they fell from a church roof while attempting to steal the lead. Arriving at the Pearly Gates, they said to St Peter:

"Can we come in?"

"No! Clear off, you cheeky devils!"
A few minutes later, God arrived:
"Where have they gone?" He asked.
"Who, those Valley boys?"
"No, you fool! The bloody gates!"

A man had to work on a Saturday afternoon forcing him to miss a rugby match between Swansea and his favourite team, Llanelli. It was on the television, so he got his girlfriend to watch it. Ten minutes after the final whistle, the man burst in.

"What was the result, luv?"

"32 to 29," she said.

"Yes, but who won?

"The one with 32," she said.

On a day trip to Barry Island, a miner approached an ice-cream van. After a pit accident, he was on crutches, had a broken arm and was wearing a neck-brace. Ordering a large cornet with chocolate sauce, the vendor asked:

"Crushed nuts?"

"No," replied the miner, "… but nearly everything else was."

There was great excitement in the small mining town of Gwaen Caer Gurwen (known locally as "GCG") when one of the sons of the town, now a Cardinal in Rome, came to visit. School children lined the streets and the emergency services formed guards of honour as he arrived at the town hall for a civic reception at which he was presented with the keys of the town and honorary membership of the NUM. After a splendid lunch, the Cardinal asked if he could visit his old Junior school and the entire entourage set off. The first classroom he entered was for eight-year-olds. He pointed at a surly brat called Johnny, and said:

"When I was your age, I sat where you are sitting right now."

"Oh, sod off!" muttered Johnny.

The children gasped, teachers fainted and dignitaries went red and purple alternately, but the Cardinal simply said:

"What did you say, young man?"

Johnny, uncowed answered:

"I said, 'Sod off'. You deaf?"

The Cardinal came and stood in front of the boy:

"Listen lad," he said, "I was born here in GCG, one of ten children. We lived in a two-bedroomed house. The old man was killed in a roof fall underground, so Mam had to take in washing to feed us. I left school at twelve and went down the pit. I worked nights regular so that I could study during the day and eventually got into theological college. After being ordained, I worked for five years in a leper colony in the Gambia and for ten years as a parish priest in Soweto. I served fifteen years with the sick and the poor in Calcutta and eventually, I was called to Rome by His Holiness the Pope. In recognition of my work, he made me a Cardinal. Now I have returned to GCG, and you tell me to 'Sod off'. No, my lad, YOU sod off!"

Tommy greets a stranger:

"Hello. How's it going, butty?"

Stranger: "Do I know you?"

"Yes, you were in the pub last night. I recognize your umbrella."

"I didn't have an umbrella in the pub last night."

"I know ... but I did."

It is sometimes forgotten that Wales has one of the best cricketing clubs in Britain, and it was one of Glamorgan's avid supporters who decided one day to introduce his girlfriend to the mysteries of the game.

On the train to Cardiff he explained: "You have two sides out

on the field, one in and one out.
Each man that's in the side that's in,
goes out and when he is out, he
comes in and the next man goes in
until he's out. When they are all out,
the side that's out comes in and the
side that's been in, goes out and
tries to get those coming in, out.
Sometimes you get men still in, who
are not out, but when both sides
have been in and out, including the
not-outs, the game is over. See?"

"It's a great shame," complained the old woman. "My grandson doesn't know how to drink or how to gamble."

"Can't be nothing wrong with that," replied her friend. "You ought to count yourself lucky."

"The thing is," explained the old woman, "he does drink and gamble, he just doesn't know *how* to drink and gamble."

Late for duty one dark night, Dai was running past the officers' mess when he collided with a general, knocking him off his feet. The enraged officer shouted:

"You clumsy oaf, do you know who I am?"

"Y-yes, sir." stuttered Dai, then added, "Do you know me, sir?"

"NO!" screamed the General.

"G-good," said Dai, and ran like hell.

Two old school friends met up after many years. One had gone to Cardiff and had done very well in business while the other had stayed at home on the family farm.

". . . And what is your son doing now?" asked the farmer.

"He's up in London studying pharmacy," came the reply.

"Duw," said his friend, "he needn't have gone all the way up there, he could have learnt to farm on our place."

An old Welsh farmer near Llanrwst had to visit the local hospital for the first time ever. Seeing his bewilderment, a sympathetic nurse approached him to ask if she could help and found he was obviously struggling with the English language. Having dealt with this situation many times in the past, she asked the old man if he wanted an interpreter to help him with the interview with the doctor. Proudly, he turned down the offer explaining:

"No thank you. I do speak two spokes, fluent."

The owner of a fish stall on Cardiff market was puzzled by the behaviour of one of his customers. He was leaning over the counter, whispering to the fish and then appeared to be listening intently.

"What are you doing, butty?" asked the fishmonger, and the customer explained:

"Well, you see, I speak several fish languages – cod, hake, haddock and so on – and I was just asking this mackerel where he was from. He told me he was from Cardigan Bay, so I asked him how things were up there as I haven't been there for ages, but he said, 'How should I know, it's *years* since I was there.' "

Jim Barker

With the National Coal Board losing millions of pounds a week in spite of the efforts of the miners, the government sent in a team of consultants to trace the problem. They started at the top by interviewing the chief executives.

"What exactly do you do?" they asked the first.

"Nothing," he replied.

"And you?" they asked the next.

"Nothing," he also replied.

"Ah!" said the expert, "This is just the sort of duplication we'd been told to expect in the mines."

Pwyll said to Twm, "That man has been sitting there doing nothing for hours."
"How do you know?" replied Twm.
"I've been sitting here watching him."

A miner was badly injured in a roof-fall underground. For weeks he lay in hospital at death's door. As his senses returned, the miner asked the doctor to explain how his injuries would affect his future.

"Well," said the doctor, "There's good news and there's bad news. I have to tell you that you will never work again."

"So what's the bad news, doctor?"

Jim Barker

The leader of a council in South Wales was instrumental in persuading a Japanese car manufacturer to build a factory in the heart of the borough. When the day arrived, the councillor was asked to perform the opening ceremony and this was followed by a tour of the plant. As he was about to leave, the president of the company handed him the keys to a brand new car.

"Thank you very much," said the councillor, "but I cannot possibly accept such a gift. People will say I'm corrupt."

The president pondered a while before suggesting that the councillor *bought* the car for a nominal fee of £5.

"Yes," mused the councillor, "that will be in order. Here's a tenner, I'll have two."

In an old farmhouse on a Welsh hillside, Evan Bevan lay dying. He called for his sons to give his final instructions for the sharing out of his beloved Welsh Blacks.

"Huw, my firstborn, you shall have half the cows. Idris, you shall have one third and Guto, my youngest, you will have one ninth."

As the old man expired, it dawned on the sons that they had 17 cows on the farm, so the division was impossible.

For days they pondered the matter, all to no avail . . . until a neighbouring farmer heard of their dilemma. Calling the three sons together he explained:

"Your father and me were friends for many years. This is a chance for me to repay his many kindnesses, so I've brought you one of my own Welsh

Blacks. Now you have 18 to share, so Huw, with a half share can have 9 cows. Idris, a third of 18 is 6 and Guto's one ninth is 2. Now 9 and 6 is 15 plus 2 adds up to 17 . . . so you all have the right number and I'll take my cow back home."

On holiday from the big city, Owen Humphries was visiting his uncle on a hill farm in Cardiganshire. Conversation did not readily flow as they had so little in common, but one evening at supper Owen, having seen the fuss on the Welsh news, asked his uncle how the lamb prices were this year. His uncle replied dolefully:

"Worse than last year, but better than next year."

An eccentric American millionaire was extremely proud of his Welsh ancestry, remote though it was and when it was found that he had an incurable disease of the brain, he lost no time in flying to Wales to consult with Dai Napper, Cardiff's foremost brain surgeon. The millionaire explained that he wanted a brain transplant – money no object. To his relief, Dai had several spare brains on ice, so off they went to chose one.

"This one here," explained the doctor, "belonged to a professor from Bangor University. A very clever man, died at the height of his powers, trampled by stampeding donkeys on Llandudno beach. Yours for £10,000."

"Maybe ... but I'm not too keen on North Walians."

"Well, how about this one? Like you, he was a successful businessman. Owned half of Swansea. Fit as a fiddle until he died on his way to work ... aged 98. Only £8,500, fitted."

"Mm ... I don't know. Too old, I think. What about that one on the top shelf?"

"Ah, well. Now you are talking big money. At least half a million, plus VAT."

"Good grief man. Whose brain is that, Einstein's?"

"Well, actually, it belonged to Dafydd Dwl, a sheep farmer from Cwm Rhiedol, drowned in his own sheep-dip, aged 102."

"So why is it more expensive than a brain from a professor, or a captain of industry?"

"That's simple . . . it's never been used."

In a rare moment of humanity, a visiting OFSTED inspector to a junior school in rural Wales, struck up a conversation with two little girls sitting at the front of the class.

"You two must be twins."

"No, sir."

"But you look identical."

"Yes, sir, but we are not twins."

"What are your names?"

"Bethan Griffiths and Olwen Griffiths, sir."

"Oh. The same family then?"

"Yes sir."

"So when are your birthdays, then?"

"Both on May 23rd, sir."

The inspector begins to suspect they are winding him up.

"So you look identical, come from the

same family and have the same birthday and still deny you are twins?"

"Yes sir. Megan, the other triplet, is off with 'flu."

During the Second World War, many foreign servicemen trained in North Wales around Harlech. Prior to their arrival, an English army officer toured the town trying to organise billets for the troops but everywhere he went, he met with refusal and returned to his base with the bad news. However, the first contingent of Free Polish Troops were all ready to move to Harlech and it fell to one of the Polish officers to try to find billets for his troops. To his amazement, having heard of the English officer's reception, nearly every house he called at offered places for his troops. In the end, he asked one of the locals why they had turned down the other officer's request:

"Ah," she replied, "we thought he wanted us to billet English soldiers."

Will Williams, on his deathbed, slipped in and out of consciousness and in one lucid moment, was startled to find himself surrounded by all the neighbouring farmers.

"What are they doing here?" he whispered to his wife.

"They've come to say 'Goodbye'," she replied.

"Oh?" said Will. "Where are they going?"

New to the parish, the vicar was telling his Cardi congregation the story of Jesus feeding the multitude:

"... and having blessed the loaves and fishes, he fed five hundred people."

"Five thousand!" hissed his wife, seated at the organ.

From behind his notes he whispered:

"I'll have enough trouble persuading this lot it was five hundred, never mind five thousand."

A customer walks into a Swansea bar.
Barman: "Bitter?"
Customer: "No. Just very, very sad."

After a long and devout life, the great Baptist preacher Jeremiah Jenkins finally arrived at the Pearly Gates. So great was his fame and goodness that God Himself greeted him and took him on a tour of Heaven. All the religions and movements were represented, living in peace and harmony, which pleased Jeremiah very much. Towards the end of the tour, however, they came across a very high brick wall and they could hear the distant sound of voices raised in song.

"Who are they, behind the wall?" asked Jeremiah.

"Shh!" said God, "It's the Calvinistic Methodists. They think they are the only ones here."

Frequently charged with nepotism, the leader of a West Wales council defended himself by quoting a religious precedent:

"After placing Adam in the Garden of Eden, God then created Eve and told Adam to choose a woman."

Dai and Gwladys were checking in at Cardiff airport. It was their first trip abroad and seeing Gwladys looked worried, Dai asked her if everything was all right.

"Oh Dai, I wish I'd brought the piano."

"Good grief, girl!" exclaimed Dai. "What the hell do you want the piano for?"

"That's where I left the passports."

At the end of a night out in the pub, a voice was heard shouting:

"Whose coat is this jacket?"

There was a break-in at the West Glamorgan council offices and the chairman was interviewed the following morning by a reporter from BBC Wales.

"Was there anything of value stolen?"

"Yes," he replied. "The results of next month's elections."

A nurse in a mid-Wales hospital refused to treat a holidaymaker on the grounds that she'd been told that she could only administer local anaesthetics.

At the scene of a car crash in a busy Cardiff street, a woman ran forward to help the victims.

She was elbowed aside by a burly man.

"Stand back love," he said commandingly. "It's okay; I've done First Aid training."

"All right," she said mildly. "But when it comes to the bit about calling for a doctor, let me know. I'll be right here."

When Moc Morgan's dog died, he was devastated. The dog had been so much part of the family that Moc, a staunch Methodist, went to his preacher and asked if the dog could be buried in the family plot.

"Good heavens, man. Bury a dog in holy ground? That would be blasphemous!" answered the minister, then seeing Moc's distress, relented somewhat and suggested he approached the local Unitarian Church who were, he believed much more liberal in such matters. Moc thought this good advice and as he turned to leave, he said:

"One more thing, Reverend. Do you think a donation of £1,000 would be appropriate for the burial service?"

The preacher paused, then said:

"Hang on a moment Moc. Was your dog a *Methodist*?"

An **Englishman and a Welshman were debating the merits of their respective countries.**

"Wales is so much friendlier than England," explained Taffy, using the following illustration.

"It's late at night. You've missed the last bus and it's pouring with rain. A total stranger stops his car and offers you a lift. He can't take you all the way home because he's short of petrol but he takes you to his own place and lights a big fire. Your clothes he takes to dry and out of the blue he produces food and as much

wine as you can drink. There's none of this sleeping on the sofa, he insists you share his bed. That's what I call real hospitality."

Impressed, the Englishman asked if it had really happened to Taffy.

"No," he replied, "but it did happen to my sister only last week."

On his deathbed, Morgan Organ, organist at the Baptist chapel for over forty years, announced that he was converting to the Calvanistic Methodists.

"But why, my love, after all these years a Baptist?" asked his wife.

"Simple," he replied, "if anyone is going to die, it may as well be one of *them*."

A sailor went into a pub in Swansea dockland with a biscuit tin in one hand and a duck under his arm. Asking the landlord's permission, he put the biscuit tin on the bar, and the duck on the biscuit tin. Immediately, the duck began to tap-dance and at the same time quacked loudly. Soon a crowd had gathered and business that night in the pub was better than it had been for weeks. Recognising the financial benefits such a novelty could bring to his business, at the end of the evening, the landlord asked the sailor if he was prepared to sell the duck. After much haggling the deal was done, and asking directions to a local guest house, the sailor left the pub.

At four o'clock in the morning, his

Jim Barker

sleep was disturbed by the arrival of the landlord:

"That bleeding duck is still dancing and quacking," cried the landlord. "The missus is going mad with the noise. How do you stop it dancing?"

"Ah!" replied the sailor, "I forgot to mention that. All you do is open the tin, and blow the candles out."

Tired of having his beer pinched everytime he went to the toilet in the Non-Pol club, a member left a note by his pint saying:

"I have spit in this."

Imagine his dismay when he returned to find someone had added: "So have I."

One night, Alderman Rhys Rees and his party secretary were busy in the local graveyard copying down all the names on the gravestones. When they got to the oldest part of the cemetery, a couple of the stones were so eroded that the names were barely legible. The secretary was all in favour of calling it a day, but the Alderman said:

"We must try and read them. This is a democracy and these two have as much right to vote as all the others in this place."

A thug from the South East went into a pub in the Rhondda. He wore a Union Jack vest, bovver boots, had a shaven head, a bone through his nose and "England for the English" tattooed on his forehead, but what the regulars noticed more than anything was the enormous Rottweiler straining at the chain held by this visitor. In the manner of such yobs, he was soon boasting of the fighting prowess of the beast and challenging anyone to put up their dog for a fight.

The landlord looked on for a long time, getting increasingly annoyed with this pushy stranger. Eventually, he said:

"Actually, I've got a dog out the back. I bet you a tenner he'd thrash yours."

Having shot his mouth off for so long,

the Englishman had no option other than to agree. On the grounds that dog fighting is a barbaric sport, unfit for civilised eyes, the yob was persuaded to let his dog go through the door to the backyard and be shut out there for five minutes.

The most horrendous noise ensued for the next five minutes, and when the back door was opened, the Rottweiler crawled back in a terrible state, battered, bitten and bleeding. His owner was visibly shocked, and asked the landlord what sort of dog could do such damage.

"Well," said the landlord, "we call them 'Long-nosed Welsh Terriers'. I believe the English call them 'Crocodiles'."

An American billionaire discovered that he had Welsh ancestry and approached a famous brain surgeon to ask if it was possible to become more Welsh by surgical means.

"Of course," replied the surgeon, sensing a fat fee for the job, "but it will involve the removal of half your brain."

Undeterred, the billionaire asked the surgeon to make the necessary arrangements. Coming round after the operation, he found the surgeon standing by his bed and looking rather sheepish:

"I have some bad news, I'm afraid." began the surgeon, "Due to some confusion between my assistant and I, we have removed all of your brain."

The American smiled reassuringly and said:

"Don't worry old bean. I feel absolutely spiffing."

Three Welsh ladies of the chapels, Olwen, Megan and Gwladys, found themselves queuing up at the Pearly Gates. St Peter was there to greet them and he explained that to prevent anybody simply *claiming* they were religious, he had to ask each of them a question before they could come in.

He began with Olwen: "Who was the first man?"

"Easy. That was Adam."

"Correct. Come in. Now Megan, who was the first woman?"

"Eve, of course."

Correct. Come in. Right Gwladys, what were Eve's first words to Adam?"

"Oh! That's a hard one."
"Correct. Come in."

During the Second World War, Swansea docks became a military target and one day Dai Duck the Diver was on the sea-bed looking for mines and unexploded bombs when the following message came through his headphones:

"Dai! Dai! You'd better come up quick. We're sinking!"

Because of the long maritime history of the region, many young men from Cardigan Bay volunteered for the Merchant Navy during the Second World

War. On his first voyage, one such lad, called Idwel, was having a terrible time of it. As soon as they left Liverpool, a terrific storm erupted and lasted for days. Long-range German bombers tried to blow them out of the water and if it had not been for a veteran, Swansea Jack, Idwel would have cracked up. Then, one pitch black night, a torpedo struck amidships. Terrified, Idwel sought out Swansea Jack.

"Quick lad!" shouted Jack. "Into the lifeboat!"

"How far away is land, Jack?" asked Idwel.

"About five miles, boy."

" Oh. That's not too bad. Which way, Jack?"

"Down!" came the ominous reply.

Dyfed was the youngest son of a hill farmer in mid-Wales. With the crisis in the farming industry it was reluctantly decided to send him to find work with the nearby Forestry Commission. The foreman explained that before he could offer Dyfed a job, he would have to prove his willingness to work hard. So saying, he handed Dyfed a chainsaw, pointed to a stand of trees nearby and told him he had to cut down at least 50 trees by four o'clock that afternoon. At the appointed time, an exhausted and disappointed Dyfed came to the foreman and explained that though he had tried his best, he had managed to cut down only 32 trees.

"Sorry lad," said the foreman, "the

rules say 50, so 50 it has to be."

As Dyfed turned to leave, the foreman added:

"Let me just check the chainsaw before you go." And he heaved on the starter cord.

As it burst into life, Dyfed shouted in terror: "Aaah! What's that noise?!"

Passions were rising high after the Young Farmers' disco, and nowhere more than in the front seat of the Land Rover occupied by Sion and Sian:

"Oh Sian!" whispered Sion. "Get in the back seat, quick!"

"No, Sion," she replied, "I'd rather stay in the front with you."

A mechanical breakdown at Porthmadoc meant that the slates, for which the area was famous, had to be loaded on to the ships by hand. One wet and windy day, Twm Bach was halfway up the gangplank when he slipped and fell into the water between ship and quay. After what seemed an eternity, he bobbed to the surface and shouted for help. A crowd gathered just in time to see him disappearing below the water again. Paralysed with horror, no one moved until he rose to the surface a second time:

"Help! Help! Throw me a rope!" shouted Twm, disappearing for the third time. Everyone stood rooted to the spot staring at the bubbles erupting on the surface where Twm

had disappeared. Then, unbelievably, he rose again and screamed:

"Throw me a rope, right now or I'll let go of the slates!"

Jacko was walking through Ynysyngharad Park in Pontypridd when he passed a man sitting on a bench. Nearby, an Alsatian dog worried a stick. Liking dogs, though his wife would not let him keep one, Jacko said to the stranger:

"'Scuse me asking, but, does your dog bite?"

"No," replied the man, "he's as gentle as a lamb."

Reassured, Jacko went over to the dog and reached out to pat him. In a flash, it turned into a ball of fury, its teeth gashing Jacko's hand and tearing a great hole in his trousers. Jumping up on to the bench to escape further attack, he shouted at the stranger:

"I thought you said your dog didn't bite."

Unruffled, the man replied:

"*That* is not *my* dog."

A man walked into a pub with a little creature on his shoulder.

"What you got there, butt?" asked the barman.

"It's my pet." replied the man. "I call him 'Tiny'."

"Why is that, then?"

"'Cos he's my newt."

Dai Sparks, a steelworker in Port Talbot, had an accident at work and his hands were badly injured. In the hospital, the operation was very difficult but the surgeon was brilliant. The next day, Dai had recovered enough to talk to him:

"Tell me, doctor," said Dai, "will I ever be able to play the piano after this?"

"Of course," reassured the surgeon, "as soon as the bandages are off."

"Well!" exclaimed Dai. "That's amazing! I couldn't play the piano before."

Dotty Williams was a game old bird, and when her grandson in Australia sent her a ticket to fly out, she jumped at the chance. She had never flown before and

was grateful for the attention given her by the stewardesses. Having reached cruising height, everyone relaxed except Dotty who was obviously in some discomfort. An observant stewardess asked if she could help, and Dotty explained that she had a pain in her ears.

"That's nothing to worry about," explained the young lady, "it's caused by pressure on the eardrums. Here, have some of this chewing gum. Most people find it helps."

Dotty thanked her, relaxed and slept for most of the flight.

On arrival in Sidney, was leaving the plane when she passed the stewardess who had been so helpful:

"Thank you for the chewing-gum. How do I get it out of my ears?"

Jim Barker

I knew I was in a truly fourth-rate Welsh hotel when I rang the desk and said:

"I've got a leak in my sink."

The clerk said:

"Well, if you must, you must. But at least rinse it out afterwards."

Pwll: So, you're not going to Venice this year?

Twm: No, I've just told you. It's Vienna we're not going to. It was Venice we didn't go to last year.

A Swansea pub landlord came up to a man standing at the bar and pointed to a cigarette end lying on the carpet.

"Excuse me. Is this yours?" he asked.

"No, no," said the man. "You can have it – you spotted it first."

A sales rep for leek-flavoured popcorn was making his last call of the week, late on Friday afternoon. A bar manager gave him a small order and he started searching through his pockets.

"What are you looking for?"

"My pen," wailed the rep. "I know I had it when I started out on Monday."

An elderly man came into the lounge bar of a Cardiff pub one day, and eased himself gently into an armchair.

"I'm a little stiff from bowling," he said, by way of explanation.

"That's all right, butt," said the barman. "We don't mind where you come from. What can I get you?"

Pub pianist: I hear you love music.
Dai: Yes, I do. But never mind,
keep on playing.

A farmer, suspecting people from the nearby village of stealing turnips from his field, put up a notice:

BEWARE. ONE OF THESE TURNIPS HAS BEEN POISONED

Next day, inspecting his sign, he saw it had been altered in two places: "One" was changed to "two", and "has" to "have".

Guto Griffiths and a colleague were consoling themselves with a beer. Trade in the town was very slow.

"I hear you had a bit of a fire at the warehouse, Charlie," said Guto.

"Quiet, Guto. That's tomorrow."

A Welsh boilerman died and went to Hell. In many ways it was similar to Cardiff and he did not feel too unhappy. One day, as the devil came by, he asked the stoker why he was feeling so cheerful.

"It's fine here," said the man. "It reminds me of my days working with the boilers. It was hotter there, but this is OK."

Irritated, the devil ordered the heat turned up in that section, and returned in a few days, to find the Welshman still smiling.

"This is good," he said. "It reminds me of the time my ship was sent out to the Persian Gulf. Now that was hot, especially down in the boiler room."

"Right," said the devil to his assistants. "If we can't make it hot enough for this fellow, we'll try the opposite. Turn

Jim Barker

everything down. I want ice everywhere. That will wipe the smile off his face."

But to his amazement, when he went to see the man, he was smiling ecstatically.

"What is now?" snarled the devil.

"I wish I was there," cried the man. "What a day! I couldn't be happier." He pointed up at the frozen roof. "Wales have won the World Cup!"

Mr and Mrs Rhys were dozing in their chairs on a Spanish hotel balcony, when they became aware of a young couple on the lawn just below. Indeed, they could hear every word the couple said to each other.

Mrs Rhys nudged her husband.

"Glyn, I think he's about to propose.

We really shouldn't be listening. Why don't you whistle, or something?"

"Why should I?" replied her husband without opening his eyes. "No one whistled to warn me."

An Englishman, a Frenchman and a Welshman were asked: "Which do you think a man needs more: a wife or a mistress?"

"Oh, a wife," said the Englishman. "Nothing beats a stable relationship."

"I say a mistress," said the Frenchman. "Those secret meetings are so exciting."

"I think a man needs both equally," said the Welshman. "That way, each thinks you're with the other, while actually you're down the pub playing snooker."

Two snooty English visitors to the Rhondda go into a local pub, rap the counter and say:

"I'll have a pint of lager."

"I'll have the same," said his friend, "... and make sure the glass is clean."

The barman returns:

"Two lagers, gentlemen. Which of you asked for the clean glass?"

Glyn: How's the family?

Wynn: Oh, pretty good. I got a new set of clubs for the wife last week.

Glyn: Hey, good trade.

On a blazing hot day in August, Glyn Rhys stepped out from the shower.

"It's so hot today," he said. "What do you think the neighbours would say if I mowed the lawn in the nude?"

"That I must have married you for your money," said his wife.

Wynn: D'you think I'm effeminate, Glyn? The wife says I am.
Glyn: I suppose you are, compared to her.